# VAMPIRE CASTLE

Anne Rooney

🜊 Crabtree Publishing Company

www.crabtreebooks.com

**Crabtree Publishing Company**
PMB 59051
350 Fifth Avenue
59th Floor
New York, New York 10118

616 Welland Avenue,
St. Catharines, Ontario
L2M 5V6

Content development by
Shakespeare Squared

www.ShakespeareSquared.com

Published by Crabtree
Publishing Company © 2008

First published in Great Britain
in 2008 by ticktock Media Ltd,
2 Orchard Business Centre,
North Farm Road,
Tunbridge Wells, Kent, TN2 3XF

ticktock project editor:
  Sophie Furse
ticktock project designer:
  Sara Greasley
ticktock picture researcher:
  Lizzie Knowles

With thanks to: Series Editors Honor Head and Jean Coppendale

Picture credits (t=top; b=bottom; c=centre; l=left; r=right):Jack
Carey/ Alamy: 20. Jim Clare/ Nature PL: 28. dpa-Film
Zephir/ dpa/ Corbis: 8. Everett Collection/ Rex Features: 23.
Ingram Publishing/ SuperStock: 12 (picture frame). Lisette Le
Bon/ SuperStock: 13. Mary Evans Picture Library/ Alamy: 25.
D. Parer & E. Parer-Cook/ Ardea: 29t. Photos 12/ Alamy: 16,
17, 22. F. Scott Schafer/ Corbis: 10. Shutterstock: OFC, 1, 2,
6-7, 7t, 11, 12 (man), 16-17 background, 14-15, 18t, 19, 21,
22-23 background, 24-25 background, 25, 26b, 26-27
background, 27, 28-29 background, 30-31 background, 31t.
Daniel Smith/ zefa/ Corbis: 18. Volker Steger/ Science Photo
Library: 26t. ticktock Media Archive: 4-5, 29b. Visual Arts
Library (London)/ Alamy: 24.

Every effort has been made to trace copyright holders, and we
apologize in advance for any omissions. We would be pleased to
insert the appropriate acknowledgments in any subsequent
edition of this publication.

Printed in Canada/012013/DM20121114

**Library and Archives Canada Cataloguing in Publication**

Rooney, Anne
    Vampire castle / Anne Rooney.

(Crabtree contact)
Includes index.
ISBN 978-0-7787-3766-7 (bound).
--ISBN 978-0-7787-3788-9 (pbk.)

    1. Vampires--Juvenile literature. I. Title. II. Series.

BF1556.R66 2008      j398'.45      C2008-901208-9

**Library of Congress Cataloging-in-Publication Data**

Rooney, Anne.
    Vampire castle / Anne Rooney.
      p. cm. -- (Crabtree contact)
Includes index.
ISBN-13: 978-0-7787-3788-9 (pbk. : alk. paper)
ISBN-10: 0-7787-3788-8 (pbk. : alk. paper)
ISBN-13: 978-0-7787-3766-7 (reinforced library binding : alk. paper)
ISBN-10: 0-7787-3766-7 (reinforced library binding : alk. paper)
    1. Vampires--Juvenile literature. I. Title. II. Series.

BF1556.R66 2008
398'.45--dc22

                                  2008006289

# CONTENTS

# VAMPIRES

Stories of vampires have been told around the world for hundreds of years.

# But do vampires really exist?

Let's read a vampire tale.

# VAMPIRE CASTLE

It's late. It's dark.
You are lost in the mountains.
The wind howls.

Should you take cover in the castle?

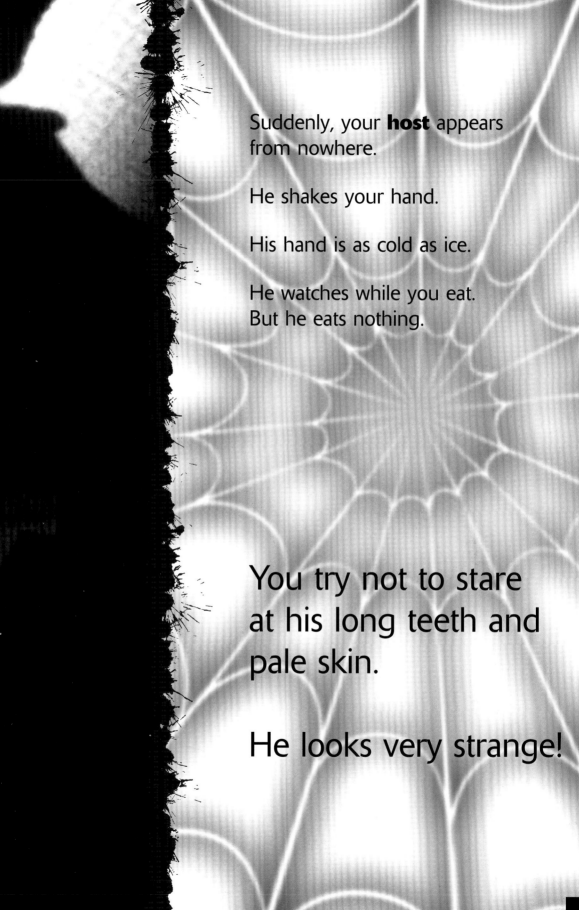

Suddenly, your **host** appears
from nowhere.

He shakes your hand.

His hand is as cold as ice.

He watches while you eat.
But he eats nothing.

You try not to stare
at his long teeth and
pale skin.

He looks very strange!

Your host leads you to a bedroom.

You are so tired that you lock the door and fall asleep right away.

In the middle of the night a noise wakes you. There is someone in your room — it's your host!

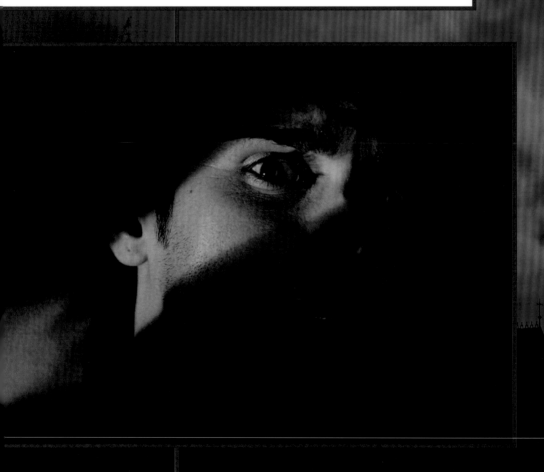

The door was locked. How did he get in?

Your host smiles at you.
His long, sharp teeth **gleam** in the moonlight.
He walks toward you.

# You back away, but...

# ...there's no escape!

You wake next morning.
Was it all a nightmare?

You feel weak. Your neck is sore.

There are bite marks on your neck!

# Your host is a vampire!

He will visit you again and again.

In the end, you will become a vampire, too — doomed to drink the blood of others forever.

# THE UNDEAD

Someone bitten by a vampire becomes
weak and pale. He or she will seem to die.

But then they will rise from their **graves** to drink blood!

Vampires are **undead**.

# There are no real vampires.

But people have been telling vampire stories for hundreds of years! There are many vampire stories, but most describe vampires in the same way.

People say a vampire sleeps during the day in its **coffin**.

A vampire must avoid sunlight — so it has very pale skin. A vampire has long, sharp, pointed teeth — to bite its **victims**!

Vampires must drink blood.
They come out only at night to
hunt for victims. Some vampires
can turn into animals, such as bats.

In some countries,
people think vampires
are not pale.

They are red from
the blood they drink!

# STOP A VAMPIRE!

In some countries, people are afraid dead bodies will turn into vampires.

They believe there are ways to stop a **corpse** from coming back as a vampire. People should:

• Tie the body's arms together.

• Nail the body to the coffin.

If you fail, the vampire will rise from its grave at night!

# Then what would you do?

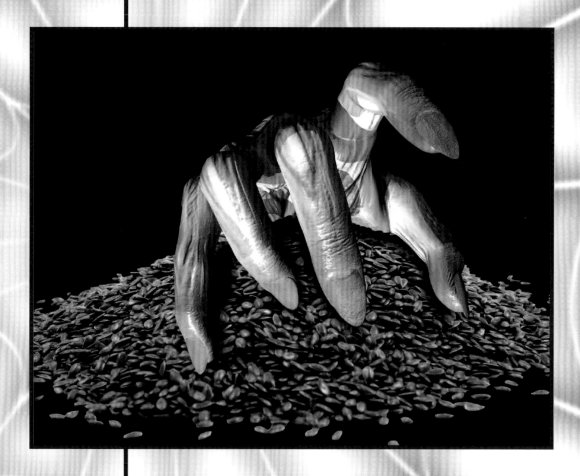

Throw rice or seeds in the vampire's path. A vampire must count every single grain before it can pass.

You need to keep the vampire busy until sunrise. Sunlight turns a vampire to dust.

the vampire returns to its grave,
ɔire hunter can destroy it.

A **crucifix** will keep vampires away.
A vampire cannot go near a crucifix.

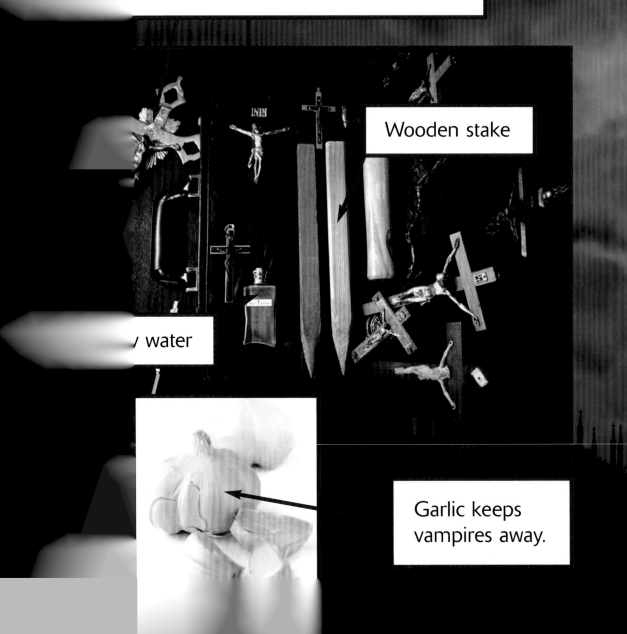

Wooden stake

ɣ water

Garlic keeps
vampires away.

**Holy water** can destroy vampires. Holy water is water that has been **blessed** by a **priest**.

A vampire hunter can hammer a wooden **stake** through a vampire's heart to destroy it.

A vampire hunter can burn a vampire's body to destroy it.

# VAMPIRES ON FILM

Vampire stories are popular. There are many movies and TV shows about vampires.

*Buffy the Vampire Slayer* is a TV show about a teenage vampire hunter. In the show, vampires can look like normal people.

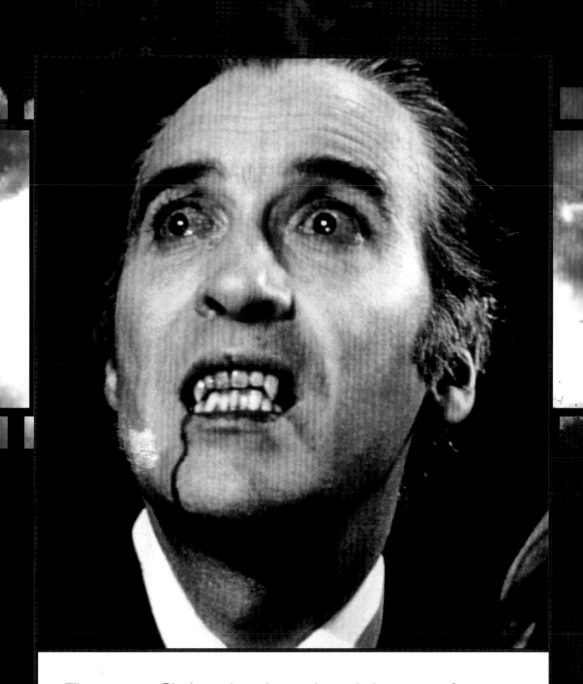

The actor, Christopher Lee played the most famous movie vampire of all – Count Dracula.

Lee wore special **contact lenses** to make his eyes look blood red.

Dracula is based on a character in a book by the writer, Bram Stoker.

# THE REAL DRACULA

Dracula's name comes from a real person called Vlad the Third of **Romania**. He was sometimes called Vlad Dracula.

The name Dracula means "son of Dracul." Dracul was the name of Vlad's father.

He was also called Vlad the Impaler. This was because he had criminals and enemies **impaled** on spikes.

Vlad lived in a castle in Romania.
Some stories say that he was a vampire.

His castle was in a forest, on a
mountain — just right for a vampire!

# VAMPIRES: FACT OR FICTION?

Why do some people believe in vampires?
Dead bodies hold a clue.

Dead people can turn dark red or purple.
They look as if they have fed on blood.

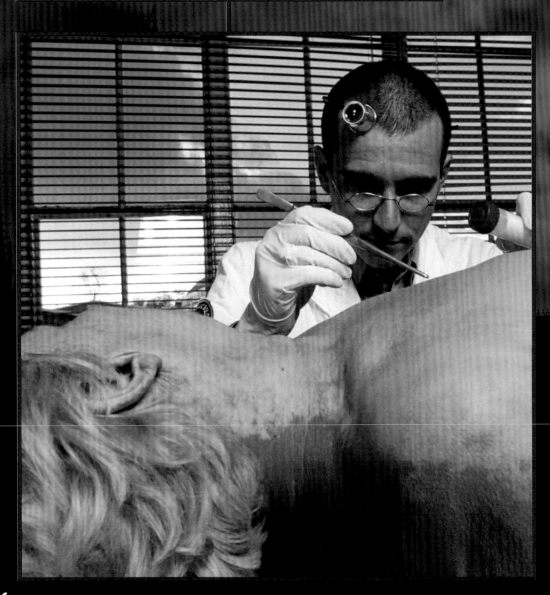

After death, the gums **shrink**. This makes the teeth look longer.

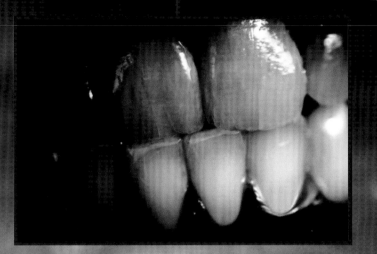

There is a rare disease that makes people easily hurt by sunlight. People with the disease stay out of the sun, so they are very pale.

The disease can also make their teeth and fingernails turn blood red.

# REAL-LIFE BLOODSUCKERS

Even though human vampires don't exist, there are vampires in the animal world. Some animals drink blood to live.

Vampire bats feed on blood.
They use their **fangs** to make tiny holes in animals. Then they lick up the blood.

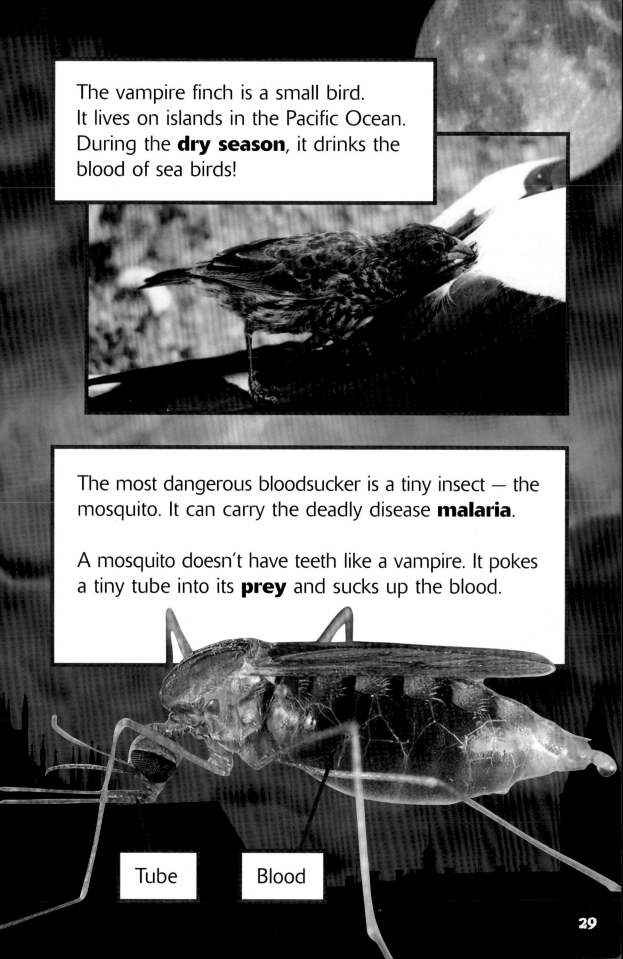

The vampire finch is a small bird. It lives on islands in the Pacific Ocean. During the **dry season**, it drinks the blood of sea birds!

The most dangerous bloodsucker is a tiny insect — the mosquito. It can carry the deadly disease **malaria**.

A mosquito doesn't have teeth like a vampire. It pokes a tiny tube into its **prey** and sucks up the blood.

Tube

Blood

# NEED-TO-KNOW WORDS

**blessed** When a priest makes something holy

**coffin** A box that holds a dead body

**contact lenses** Small round pieces of plastic put into the eye to help a person see

**corpse** A dead body

**crucifix** An image or figure of Jesus on the cross

**dry season** A time of year when not much rain falls

**fang** A long, sharp tooth

**gleam** A small flash of light reflected from a shiny surface

**grave** A hole in the ground where a dead body is buried

**host** A person who lets guests stay in their home

**impale** To push a sharp stake or spike through something

**malaria** A disease caused by the bite of some mosquitoes

**prey** An animal that is hunted by another animal as food

**priest** Someone whose job is to lead religious services

**Romania** A country in Europe

**shrink** To get smaller

**stake** A wooden stick with a point at one end

**undead** A person who is dead but can still move around

**victim** A person that something bad happens to

# VAMPIRES AROUND THE WORLD

- In China, there are stories of a vampire called a kuangshi. It has bright red eyes, sharp fangs, and is covered in green hair.

- In India, stories tell of a female vampire called a churel. It has a black tongue and back-to-front feet.

- In Malaysia, there are stories of a vampire called a bajang. This is a demon that can be kept in a jar and used to hurt enemies.

# VAMPIRES ONLINE

## Websites
*http://library.thinkquest.org/5482/*
Some general information on vampire stories

*http://science.howstuffworks.com/vampire.htm*
The history of vampire stories around the world

*http://kids.nationalgeographic.com/Animals/CreatureFeature/Vampire-bat*
Facts about vampire bats

# INDEX